Milano

Text by
Debora Munda

Mi viaje a Italia
Sept 2006

the Da Vinci Code
Trail

Roma
Milan
Suiza
Paris
Londres
Edimburgo

Electa

Table of contents

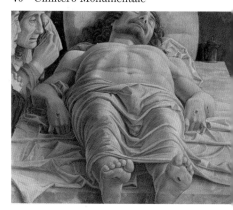

Map
of the city
on page 126

The Heart of the City

Piazza del Duomo

This square is the heart of the city and the symbol of Milan. The outcome of centuries of transformation(s) and incessant demolition and reconstruction, the square as we see it today owes its appearance to work that began in the second half of the nineteenth century.

The Milan cathedral – or Duomo – and the monument dedicated to Victor Emanuel II are set in the centre of a large rectangle that stretches from Via Mercanti to Piazza della Scala and to Piazza San Babila. The north porticoes are broken up by the arch that is the majestic entrance to the Galleria Vittorio Emanuele II. Set facing each other on the opposite side are the two pavilions of the Arengario – unmistakable Fascist architecture – now used to house contemporary art exhibits.

Beneath the square is a vast system of underground areas connected with an enormous metro station linking Line 1 (red) and Line 3 (yellow). The work to build Line 1 unearthed some of the ruins of the ancient basilica of Santa Tecla and Santa Maria Maggiore, as well as the extraordinary octagonal baptistery of *San Giovanni ad Fontes*, built by St. Ambrose.

Piazza Duomo, north porticoes, entrance to the Galleria Vittorio Emanuele II.

Duomo

Gian Galeazzo Visconti initiated construction of the cathedral in 1386, but it was not completed until the mid-nineteenth century. Devoted to the Nascent Mother, the new cathedral was built over what was Santa Maria Maggiore. The work involved architects and sculptors of different cultures, symbolizing never-ending labour. The prized marble with grey-pink veining used to build the cathedral came from the quarries of Candoglia, located near Lake Maggiore. It was transported to Milan by water, across the lake and then down the Ticino River and the Navigli canals to the dock of the "little lake" near the ancient market of Verziere.

The cathedral, built in the Flamboyant Gothic style, is distinguished by nearly 3500 statues and by its spires. It also reflects the continuous search for technical concepts that had never been used before, such as the extraordinary size of the windows of the apse, the height of the tiburium and its horizontal layout. The oldest part is the apse: the structure, designed by Frenchman Nicolas de Bonaventure and built by Filippino degli Organi, is decorated with priceless sculptures. The façade is the most recently constructed part of the cathedral and a closer look clearly reveals two different concepts, the upper portion above the first order

Duomo, the tiburium with the gilt statue of the Madonnina, devoted to Our Lady.

of windows and the central balcony were completed during the Napoleonic Age and feature stiff Gothic forms, whereas the lower part – including the five entrances and the wide fasciae with bas-reliefs – is a Baroque complex designed by Cerano.

The interior is powerfully evocative, with light filtering through the stained-glass windows (the oldest panels, dating from the fifteenth century, can be found mainly in the windows of the right aisle) and the soaring height of the 52 colossal polystyle pillars, which sustain the vaults over the five aisles. In place of the capitals, there is a series of niches with statues, a spectacular device that breaks up the ascendant movement of the pillars. The proportions are remarkable: the cathedral is 158 metres (518´) long and 93

metres (305´) wide at the transept, it covers an area of 11,700 square metres (126,000 sq.ft), and the vault of the tiburium rises to a height of 69 metres (226´). Extensive work was carried out under Pellegrino Tibaldi while St. Charles Borromeo was archbishop of Milan (1562-1584): the inlaid floor, side altars, the presbytery and the choir, and the tabernacle of the baptistery at the beginning of the left aisle. The Duomo sculptures are fascinating. Along the right aisle, we immediately come to the tomb of Archbishop Ariberto d'Intimiano, followed by various stone tablets of historical interest and the tomb of the merchant Marco Carelli, built during the Late Gothic period by Filippino degli Organi and Jacopino da Tradate. On the right side of the transept, which is decorated with windows dating from the fifteenth and sixteenth centuries, is the funerary monument of Gian Giacomo Medici, the work of Leone Leoni. To the front is an altar by Bambaia,

*Duomo, close-up
of the windows
of the apse.*

*Interior of the
Duomo: the nave.*

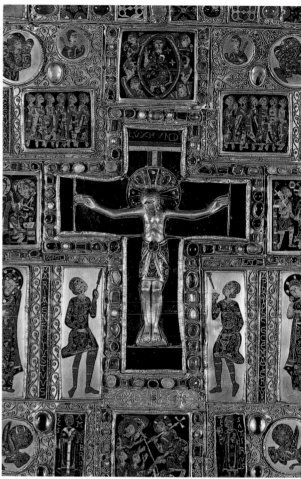

with a high-relief altarpiece portraying the *Presentation in the Temple*. Next to it is a statue by Marco d'Agrate, representing *St. Bartholomew flayed*. Across from the presbytery is the late-sixteenth-century complex ordered by St. Charles Borromeo. The complex includes two enormous organs with painted doors, two suspended pulpits on the entrance pillars, the domed tabernacle and the carved walnut choir.

The ambulatory leads to the oldest part of the cathedral. The portal of the south sacristy, the work of German and Burgundian masters, is at the beginning of this section on the right side. Across from the sacristy is the entrance leading down to the rooms beneath the choir. The circular crypt, clad in coloured marble, is connected with the *Scurolo di San Carlo*, a small octagonal chapel by Francesco Maria Richini (1606). The vestibule of this funerary chapel is connected, in turn, with the treasures of the cathedral: a single room houses exquisite liturgical furnishings dating from the fourth to the twentieth century. The most important works here are the marvellous *Ariberto Evangelarium*, a masterpiece of eleventh-century Lombard goldsmithery with enamel work and filigree,

and the *capsella* of St. Nazarius, a fourth-century reliquary with relief work done in a classical style but featuring Christian subjects. The reliquary is the work of Roman goldsmiths who also worked for the imperial court.

Proceeding along the ambulatory – with spectacular seventeenth-century organ doors, the sculptures of the enclosure around the choir and the immense stained-glass windows of the apse – we come to the left transept. In the centre is the Trivulzio candelabrum, a splendid and highly elaborate bronze masterpiece done in the early thirteenth century by the Lorena or Mosan goldsmiths.

The stairway to the terraces is located outside on the left side, so that visitors can complete their tour of the cathedral with a view of the upper portions of the building. This tour offers visitors a close look at the countless ancient sculptures, including the Amadeo spire and the Carelli spire, located over the ambulatory. The latter is the oldest spire, and it is topped by a statue of Gian Galeazzo Visconti, portrayed as St. George.

The main spire dates from 1769 and, with the popular statue of the Madonnina (the work of Giuseppe Perego, 1774), it rises to a height of 108 metres (354´).

Trivulzio
candelabrum, early
thirteenth century.
Duomo,
left transept.

Palazzo Reale

Palazzo Reale – the Royal Palace – was built during the Middle Ages and it was the residence of the Torriani, Visconti and Sforza families. Its current appearance dates from the late eighteenth century, when Empress Marie Thérèse of Austria organized a "competition by invitation" open to the leading architects of the period in order to adapt the complex to house the governor.

Giuseppe Piermarini (1734-1808), a student of Vanvitelli and a representative of Milan's Neoclassical movement, won the competition and his project, which exploited and modified the existing structures, was used. This work embellished the palace with sumptuous stuccowork and gilt decorations, making it the perfect backdrop for the lavish social events that were to be held there. In 1936, the right wing was demolished and it has now been replaced with Palazzo dell'Arengario. Subsequently, the tragic bombings in 1943 caused heavy damage: the ceiling of the lovely Room of the Caryatids was demolished, the Hayez fresco decorating the room was completely lost, and many of the works in the rooms of the palace were damaged by explosions as well as bad weather.

Royal Palace, the façade facing the Duomo.

Royal Palace, interior, the staircase to the piano nobile, where exhibits are held regularly.

Palazzo dell'Arengario, exterior.

Bell tower of San Gottardo in Corte, fourteenth century.

Palazzo dell'Arengario

The intricate history of the planning and architecture of Piazza del Duomo took an important turn in the 1930s with the construction of Palazzo dell'Arengario, which was designed by Marcello Piacentini and decorated with bas-reliefs by Arturo Martini.

A perfect example of Constructivist architecture – simple and grand, but also somewhat rhetorical – the Arengario ultimately became the permanent venue of the Museo del Novecento, the museum of twentieth-century art.

San Gottardo in Corte

Once used as the palatine chapel of the Visconti residence, this church dating from the Middle Ages is incorporated in the rear section of Palazzo Reale. The bell tower and apse are all that remain of the fourteenth-century Gothic structure that was the work of architect Francesco Pecorari. Inside, there is part of a fresco taken from the bell tower, and this work depicting the *Crucifixion* is valuable evidence of Giotto's influence on fourteenth-century Lombard painting. This is the "bell tower of the Duomo", as the cathedral lacks one.

Piazza Mercanti and the Broletto Nuovo

Intimate, discreet, secluded: these words provide a perfect description of this little square, the mediaeval heart of Milan. This little corner of the old city has miraculously been preserved, off the beaten track and away from noisy city traffic. The square is what remains following the work done in 1867-1877 to create a long roadway to connect Piazza del Duomo with the northern part of the city. The piazza was originally quadrangular, with the Broletto Nuovo – or new town hall – in the centre and six arched passageways leading to the city's six main gates. Palazzo della Ragione, also known as the Broletto Nuovo, was built between 1228 and 1233. The building housed the city magistracies, responsible for settling disputes. The Broletto Nuovo is composed of three rows of arches set on pillars and an upper floor in terracotta, with three-light windows. The second floor was added in the late eighteenth century. The picturesque Loggia degli Osii, built in the early fourteenth century, overlooks Piazza Mercanti, and in front of the Loggia there is a sixteenth-century well. The columns and trabeation were added to the well in the eighteenth century.

Loggia degli Osii with the sixteenth-century well, known as the "stone of the bankrupt merchants".

Broletto Nuovo, 1228-1233.

Galleria Vittorio Emanuele II, 1865-1877.

Galleria Vittorio Emanuele II

The gallery links Piazza del Duomo and Piazza della Scala. The plans drawn up in 1859 initially called for a road honouring Austrian emperor Franz Joseph. Work began in 1865 under the supervision of Giuseppe Mengoni, but just before the gallery was inaugurated Mengoni was killed when he fell from the scaffolding. Completed in 1877, the gallery was dedicated to the King of Italy, Victor Emanuel II.

The gallery has four arms branching from a central octagon, and it is covered with vaulting made of iron and glass. Visitors can admire twenty-four statues portraying illustrious Italians, set in the mezzanines of the octagon and at the sides of the four entrances. Six of them are larger than the others: representing Alessandro Volta, Michelangelo, Galileo, Camillo Cavour, Leonardo da Vinci and Pier Capponi. They are the work of sculptor Cesare Magni.

In the past, the gallery would be illuminated at sundown by 600 gas flames. They were lit by a steam device with two hot wicks that, hooked to two overhead rails, moved along the gallery to light the flames.

With its elegant atmosphere and the stores lining the interior, the gallery quickly became the rendezvous of the Milanese and thus one of the city's most prestigious symbols. Because of the building's charming appearance and extensive space, the gallery is now used for cultural and commercial events as well as fashion shows.

Piazza della Scala

This square, typical of the city-planning work of the late nineteenth century, is surrounded by monumental buildings whose style was inspired by the simple but noble façade of the Teatro alla Scala. The layout was designed by Luca Beltrami, who also designed the façade of Palazzo Marino and the two symmetrical buildings of the Banca Commerciale along the sides. The impressive monument to Leonardo da Vinci, in the centre of the square, is by Cesare Magni (1872).

Palazzo Marino

The seat of the municipal government and of the mayor's offices, this magnificent building was designed by Galeazzo Alessi for banker Tommaso Marino. The work began in 1553, but the main façade, across from the opera house, dates from the nineteenth century.

The rear façade is an excellent example of classicism, with overlaid architectural elements that create a powerful vertical line. The courtyard, crowded with niches, pillars, reliefs, tables and herms, is also noteworthy.

Galleria Vittorio Emanuele II, close-up of the dome.

Piazza della Scala with the entrance to the Galleria Vittorio Emanuele II.

Piazza della Scala with the façade of Palazzo Marino and the monument to Leonardo da Vinci.

Giuseppe Verdi and La Scala

La Scala represents the aristocracy of Italian opera, as demonstrated by its long list of premieres of famous operas written by the leading composers in the history of music.

On a curious note: La Scala was "spawned" by fire. Located inside the building now referred to as Palazzo Reale was the Teatro di Palazzo Ducale, which was destroyed by fire in February 1776. Prior to this theatre, there was another one, the Teatro Ducale, but it burned to the ground in 1708. Strangely, it had been built in place of the Regio Ducale Teatro, which likewise burned down in 1669.

After three fires in the same building, Marie Thérèse of Austria decided to have the new Teatro Grande – as it was originally to be called – built elsewhere, albeit nearby. Consequently, a far more important theatre was rapidly constructed, designed by architect Giuseppe Piermarini, and it was inaugurated on the evening of 3 August 1778: this was the Teatro alla Scala. To protect it from fire, Piermarini designed an ingenious hydraulic machine, but fortunately there has never been any need to test its effectiveness. La Scala, which was restructured during the nineteenth century, was partially destroyed by bombs in 1943. It was promptly rebuilt and its reopening, with a memorable concert conducted by Arturo Toscanini, was hailed as the symbol of Milan's post-war revival.

Museo Teatrale alla Scala

It was inaugurated on 8 March 1913. The museum was named after the opera house because its halls are located in the same building. The museum houses mementos, portraits, busts, medals and laurels of musicians,

Interior of the Teatro alla Scala following the bombing on 15 August 1943.

The interior of the Teatro alla Scala, facing the boxes.

orchestra conductors, stage designers, singers and dancers who have been part of the history of this musical "shrine".
Two special rooms also hold all the mementos of Giuseppe Verdi, Milan's favourite composer. The bronze bust of Verdi and the terracotta one of his wife Giuseppina Strepponi are the magnificent work of sculptor Vincenzo Gemito. The Museo Teatrale alla Scala is currently housed on Corso Magenta, as the opera house is being restored.

Giuseppe Verdi

Verdi is an important figure in the history of the opera house and of Milan itself. He epitomizes sweeping emotion and boundless passion, the spoken word that is no longer sufficient and discovers its fullest expression in the power of song. With him, music was transformed from the pleasure of the spirit to an instrument of social and political confrontation. Verdi thus became the ideal portrayer of the city's passion. His name resounded during Milan's most difficult years. The episode of the final days of Austrian domination is enlightening. Street urchins would scribble "Viva Verdi" on the walls of city houses, as an acrostic referring not to the composer but to "Vittorio Emanuele Re D'Italia" [Victor Emanuel King of Italy].

Giuseppe Verdi, Museo Teatrale alla Scala, photographic collection.

Vittorio Rota, sketch for Scene I, Act II, of Verdi's Il Trovatore, 1902. Museo Teatrale alla Scala.

Carlo Ferrario, "Interior of Sachs' shop", sketch for Act III of Richard Wagner's The Mastersingers of Nuremberg, 1898-1899. Museo Teatrale alla Scala.

Teatro alla Scala

Since its inauguration (on 3 August 1778 with a performance of Antonio Salieri's opera *L'Europa riconosciuta*), La Scala has been the location for the city's opera and ballet season. It was commissioned by Marie Thérèse of Austria from the architect Giuseppe Piermarini, and built between 1776 and 1778. The name came from the fourteenth-century church of Santa Maria della Scala, which was demolished to make room for the theatre. The exterior is simple and restrained, typical of architecture at the time of Marie Thérèse.

The façade pediment is decorated with a relief of Apollo's chariot, and it is preceded by a portico that allowed those arriving by carriage to have "sheltered" access to the theatre. The auditorium horseshoe has four tiers of boxes, a circle and upper circle, seating in total an audience of 3600. Its acoustics are considered perfect.

The furnishing is neoclassical, subsequent to the interventions by Giovanni Perego and Alessandro Sanquirico, who created the great chandelier. The stage, which was enlarged in 1814, is still involved in work to adapt it to state-of-the-art stage technology.

The theatre has its own museum annex – Museo Teatrale alla Scala – arranged in fourteen rooms housing mementos, testimonies, paintings, objects, artist autographs, instruments that map out the history of the opera house and, in particular, episodes apropos the personalities linked to La Scala.

Giuseppe Piermarini, Teatro alla Scala, 1776-1778.

Pellegrino Tibaldi, Church of San Fedele, 1569-1579.

The sculpture Il Sole by Arnaldo Pomodoro, in Piazza Meda.

Piazza San Fedele

One of Milan's loveliest squares is a nook of tranquillity, its centre decorated with Francesco Barzaghi's monument to Alessandro Manzoni. The rear façade of Palazzo Marino and the San Fedele church façade are both in sixteenth-century classical style, as ordered by Cardinal Borromeo, who commissioned it to be built on the site of Santa Maria in Solariolo. It was designed by the most famous architect of the period, Pellegrini (Pellegrino Tibaldi). Work began in 1569 and the inauguration was in 1579. The remains of the martyrs Fidelis and Carpophorus were brought from Arona for the occasion, and were then housed under the high altar. Piazza San Fedele is an "ancient place" and a historic treasure: it was here that the troops of the Emperor Henry VII began their massacre of the Milanese involved in the rebellion at the time of the Torriani family. The family's houses were demolished, and they are now recalled in the street name Via Case Rotte [the street of destroyed houses].

The other two sides of the piazza were occupied by the Teatro Manzoni and the famous "Bella Venezia" hotel, whose guests included Goldoni and Mazzini. Bombings in 1943 destroyed them and they have been replaced by new buildings.

Piazza Meda

The 1930s buildings are the chief feature. In 1980 a sculpture by Arnaldo Pomodoro was installed at its centre: a great bronze disc, four metres (13´) in diameter, symbolizing the sun.

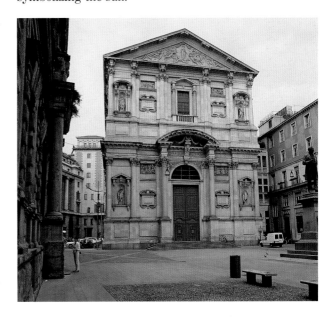

Casa degli Omenoni

This is in the street of the same name, between Palazzo Marino and Teatro alla Scala. The name comes from the Milanese dialect word (*omenon*) describing Antonio Abbondio's eight caryatids, the famous telamon sculptures that decorate the façade of sculptor Leone Leoni's sixteenth-century house.

This house was the first place to host the famous series of *Disegni di Machina et delle Arti Secrete et altre cose di Leonardo da Vinci* [Leonardo's drawings of machines and secret arts and other things], collected by Pompeo Leoni in the decade from 1580 to 1590. The fabulous collection of drawings was then sold to the Marquis Galeazzo Arconati in 1637 and donated to the Ambrosiana museum where it is stored as the *Codex Atlanticus*, one of the most important testimonies to the genius of Leonardo.

Piazza Belgioioso

A surviving niche of neoclassical Milan opens with an outer court in front of the ample colonnaded façade of Palazzo Belgioioso designed by architect Giuseppe Piermarini and giving the square its name. An arcade separates the square from modern Piazza Meda. Narrow Via Omenoni is opposite Palazzo Belgioioso, and the bottom of the piazza is closed on one side by Alessandro Manzoni's house.

Alessandro Manzoni's House

Alessandro Manzoni bought the fifteenth-century building in April 1813 from the Viennese De Felber family. A year later he moved there, with his wife Enrichetta Blondel, and lived there for almost sixty years.

The writer probably chose the mansion for its quiet location and huge garden. It now belongs to the Banca Commerciale and looks out across Piazza Belgioioso, with the palazzo of the same name. When Piazza Belgioioso was refurbished, between 1861 and 1864, the façade of Manzoni's house was also restored, with terracotta decoration, to a design by the architect Andrea Boni.

After the writer's death, the house changed hands several times: for this reason a great many relics and furnishings were lost, and the appearance of the building was changed.

Restoration undertaken from 1961 to 1965 refurbished the structure and much of the apartment, including the façade decorations in terracotta, found in a country garden. The Museo Manzoniano is now housed here.

Poldi Pezzoli Museum

The museum is an elegant palazzo on Via Manzoni. After the death of its founder, Gian Giacomo Poldi Pezzoli (1879), its rooms were opened to the public. The exhibit path begins on the ground floor, which includes the armoury, re-

Casa degli Omenoni, detail of two telamons that decorate the sixteenth-century façade.

Piazza Belgioioso: on the left is Palazzo Belgioioso, designed by Giuseppe Piermarini; opposite is Alessandro Manzoni's house.

House of Alessandro Manzoni, the façade looking onto Piazza Belgioioso.

Poldi Pezzoli Museum, Via Manzoni.

cently renovated by Arnaldo Pomodoro, resembling a unique sculpture-installation, library and collection of antique lace and fabrics. The marvellous "hunt" carpet, a Persian masterpiece woven in Tabriz in the early sixteenth century, is kept in a special display cabinet.

An elegant stairway with fountain leads to the piano nobile. The three small rooms dedicated to the Lombards are on the immediate left. The works collected here offer a full overview of Lombard paintings from the Late Gothic to the Renaissance, from the gold background panels by Cristoforo Moretti and Gottardo Scotti to the masters of the second half of the 1400s such as Vincenzo Foppa (*Madonna with Child*), Bergognone and Bernardino Zenale. There are also important works by Giovanni Antonio Boltraffio, Cesare da Sesto and Bernardino Luini.

The museum's chief room is the Salone Dorato, hung with famous Renaissance works like Pollaiolo's *Portrait of a Lady*, Botticelli's *Madonna with the Book* and *Deposition*, Mantegna's *Madonna with Child* and *San Nicolò da Tolentino* by Piero della Francesca.

There follows a sequence of rooms that includes the Viscontea collection, the Falck collection, with extremely important antique clocks, and a room dedicated to the work of Fra Galgario.

The visit then includes a number of rooms that have, in part, retained their nineteenth-century appearance: the Gabinetto Dantesco is one of the few rooms in the house to have survived with its original decoration and (it) was the count's private studio. Some of the original furnishings have been preserved, designed specifically for the room by four artists, as well as the stained-glass opus known as the *Trionfo di Dante* [*Triumph of Dante*], by Giuseppe Bertini.

Sandro Botticelli, Madonna with Child *(Madonna with the* Book*), 1480. Poldi Pezzoli Museum.*

Francesco Guardi, Gondola on the lagoon *(Grey lagoon), 1770. Poldi Pezzoli Museum.*

Following pages
Vincenzo Foppa, Madonna with Child, *mid-fifteenth century. Poldi Pezzoli Museum.*

Antonio Benci, known as Pollaiolo, Portrait of a young woman, *mid-fifteenth century. Poldi Pezzoli Museum.*

Vittore Ghislandi, known as Fra Galgario, Gentleman with Cocked Hat, 1745 circa. Poldi Pezzoli Museum.

An early sixteenth-century Persian carpet called The "Hunt". Poldi Pezzoli Museum.

Two details of The "Hunt" carpet. Poldi Pezzoli Museum.

Velasca Tower

The Tower was designed by the architecture group BBPR (Banfi, Belgioioso, Peressutti and Rogers). Built between 1956 and 1960, it is considered one of the most important post-war buildings. This 26-storey skyscraper houses offices and residential accommodations, and it widens from the 18th floor, making it reminiscent of an ancient tower. Its name derives from that of the piazza, originally opened in 1651 by the Spanish governor, Juan de Velasco.

Studio BBPR,
Torre Velasca.

San Nazaro (or Basilica degli Apostoli)

The architectural overview of this building looking on-to Corso di Porta Romana shows three moments of construction: Romanesque sections were added to the original base (eleventh-century tiburium, apse, side portal) and two large Renaissance chapels. The basilica was restored after being damaged by bombings.

The animated left flank is preceded by the sixteenth-century Santa Caterina chapel, and behind this, the tiburium. The church has no façade. The entrance is to the Trivulzio chapel, a separate building, from the opening in the Corso. It was begun in 1512, designed by Bramantino as the burial place for the Marshal Gian Giacomo Trivulzio and his family, but the exterior was never completed and this appears as a block cadenced by pilaster strips. The octagonal interior reveals the Bramantesque source of inspiration in severe, magnificent forms. Above there are the Trivulzio sepulchres, and below the chapel extends down to a crypt supported by a single, central pillar.

Below is the basilica with a single nave and a vast presbytery. The "little" basilica of San Lino is located between the choir and the sacristy: it is a small tenth-century section with fragments of Romanesque frescoes. The left transept leads to the spacious Santa Caterina chapel with its radiant Renaissance architecture inspired by Bramante.

San Nazaro,
the apse.

Piazza Santo Stefano

The piazza retains in part its nature of a people's square, with two religious buildings forming a right angle: Piazza Santo Stefano to the left, San Bernardino alle Ossa to the right, and the façade of the church of Santo Stefano. The collegiate church of Santo Stefano in Brolo is a late-1500s reconstruction of a Romanesque building, preceded in ancient times by a quadriporticus, of which only an isolated pillar has survived. The complex, formed by the façade and the belfry, is a fine example of restrained Milanese Baroque. Inside are many seventeenth-century canvases.

Ca' Granda – State University

Home of the State University, it is one of the most significant interventions left by the Sforza era at an architectural, city planning and social level. The design, which Francesco Sforza entrusted to the Tuscan architect Antonio Averlino, called "Filarete", initiated one of the greatest and most well-equipped hospitals in Europe. The building originally included a right wing, with a central cross vault that created four symmetrical courtyards. This initial fifteenth core was then integrated with the central element, with the portal that opens onto the great court. The work then continued on the left wing, which was finished in the early nineteenth century, with a great deal of rebuilding to repair the destruction caused by war and to set up the rooms for university use. The various phases of building can be identified in the brick façade, which is almost 300 metres long (985´). The right wing, with a Renaissance loggia continuing along the side and a central pediment, corresponds to the Filarete building. The central part of the façade has great, two-light lancet windows and has a huge portal with statues, leading into the spacious inner courtyard, surrounded by large arched porticoes and loggias, decorated with reliefs and busts.

Piazza Santo Stefano, to the left, San Bernardino alle Ossa, to the right, the façade of the church of Santo Stefano.

Ca' Granda, the central section of the façade.

Ca' Granda, detail of the two-light lancet windows.

Palazzo Sormani

The location of the Biblioteca Civica [civic library] is an example of what is defined as "barocchetto", the Lombard version of Rococo.

The main façade, with its curved coping, is by Francesco Croce (1736); thirty years later Benedetto Alfieri created the rear prospect that looks out into the garden.

Piazza Cinque Giornate

Piazza Cinque Giornate is notable for its monument by Giuseppe Grandi. The "Saviour" column was already present. This was a "station column" commissioned by the confraternities of the Milanese districts and mostly demolished in 1786 to make way for road improvements.

Francesco Croce, façade of Palazzo Sormani, 1736.

Piazza Cinque Giornate with its monument by Giuseppe Grandi.

*Rotonda
della Besana.*

*Rotonda della
Besana, inner
portico, with church
at the centre.*

Rotonda della Besana

The multilobated building is also known as "Foppone dell'ospedale". It was actually built in about 1695 for burying the dead from Ca' Granda, and it has an unusual appearance of portico with a church in the centre (by Attilio Arrigoni, Francesco Croce and Carlo Francesco Raffagno). Beneath the portico, around the church of San Michele, there are numerous, very deep crypts, where the dead were brought and walled up (approxi-

mately 150,000) until 1752. The corpses stayed there until 1952, when the place was finally emptied and reclaimed. The Rotonda also had other uses.

It became a hospital for isolating contagious patients during the 1870-1871 smallpox epidemic; from the turn of the twentieth century until 1940 it was the hospital laundry. In about 1960, the inner part was turned into public gardens, and the church became an arts and culture centre.

Palazzo di Giustizia

A sensational example of Fascist architecture, designed by Marcello Piacentini in 1932.

The massive structure is covered in marble slabs and preceded by a ramp of stairs. The interior is decorated in reliefs and mosaics, the work of some of Italy's finest artists of the Thirties, including Mario Sironi, Gino Severini and Arturo Martini.

In order to build the Palace of Justice, a dense zone of religious buildings and ancient convents was demolished.

San Pietro in Gessate

Built in the mid-fifteenth century, this church has retained its Late Gothic traits, despite several later modifications (portal). The interior, with a nave and two aisles, is cadenced by stone columns and ogival arches. The chapels along the left side retain frescoes by Montorfano; in the right transept there is a fresco by Bergognone *Funeral of St. Martin*, detached from its original housing. The left transept is occupied by the Grifi Chapel, frescoed in 1490 by Butinone and Zenale.

Marcello Piacentini, Palazzo di Giustizia, 1932.

San Pietro in Gessate, mid-fifteenth century.

Ambrogio da Fossano, called "Bergognone", frescoes in the chapter house at Santa Maria della Passione.

Gaudenzio Ferrari, Last Supper, *1541-1543. Santa Maria della Passione.*

Santa Maria della Passione

After the Duomo, this is Milan's biggest church and may be considered a brief anthology of Lombard Renaissance architecture and of sixteenth- and seventeenth-century painting. The church was designed in the late fifteenth century by Giovanni Battagio and originally had a Greek cross layout, with an octagonal cupola that had four, symmetrical apse wings. This layout can still be seen from careful observation of the apse section, surmounted by a tiburium with niches, completed by Cristoforo Lombardi. In 1573, Martino Bassi designed the front complex, with a nave and two aisles, and side chapels. The façade dates back to the early eighteenth century.

The brightly lit interior has retained its furnishings from the sixteenth and seventeenth centuries. The decoration, as a whole, is particularly sumptuous and precious, including several extremely important paintings.

The left transept is enhanced by Gaudenzio Ferrari's *Last Supper*; the right transept has the altarpiece with the *Deposition*, probably painted by Bernardino Luini.

The niche to the right of the presbytery leads into the Santa Maria della Passione Museum. The Chapter House is decorated with a cycle by Bergognone, one of the most important masters of Renaissance painting.

The fashion streets

Piazza San Babila

The square is the result of city planning interventions undertaken in the Thirties and is demarcated by great porticoed buildings, taking its name from the ancient basilica of San Babila (eleventh century), located on the corner of Corso Monforte and preceded by Giuseppe Robecco's seventeenth-century column.

The basilica was probably built over an existing fifth-century version and founded by St. Laurence I, then rebuilt in Neo-Romanesque form between 1853 and 1905. What we see today is an example of a late-nineteenth-century Milanese refurbishment.

Piazza San Babila towards Corso Vittorio Emanuele on the right, and Corso Europa on the left.

San Babila, façade with bell tower.

Via Montenapoleone.

Palazzo Bagatti Valsecchi.

Via Montenapoleone

Milan, like all great cities around the world, is obviously not just an art city: its international fame is also linked to the streets that form the "fashion quadrilateral", with its concentration of clothing and accessory stores. Via Montenapoleone is the most famous, and the biggest names in Italian high fashion have their storefronts here. An afternoon is insufficient for seeing all the shops. Fortunately, weary shoppers can take a break in one of the smart local cafés, to sample a coffee or a pastry. On the left, from Via Manzoni, in the direction of Corso Matteotti, we find Via Borgospesso, Via Santo Spirito, Via Gesù and Via Sant'Andrea, which all finish at aristocratic Via della Spiga. This is the composition of this eighteenth/nineteenth-century quarter, which has survived virtually intact and is the location of several refined museums, housed in noble buildings.

Palazzo Bagatti Valsecchi

This is an example of "period" architecture of the late nineteenth century, where the palazzo pays homage to Renaissance style: the effect is achieved by using antique material mixed with imitations. The mansion, which is now the Bagatti Valsecchi museum, was home to the brothers Fausto and Giuseppe Bagatti Valsecchi from the 1880s. The two brothers belonged to a family of the Milanese nobility, who studied law but dedicated their lives to their passion for the arts and forming their collection of objects. The Bagatti Valsecchi brothers dreamed of creating a noble Renaissance residence, but they did not pursue this dream by imitating a single model: for their palazzo they referred to and revisited outstanding examples to create a Renaissance style filtered through nineteenth-century sensitivity, in which the Bagatti Valsecchi hallmark always emerges.

The two brothers concentrated on works executed between the fifteenth and sixteenth century; they collected fragments of architecture, wall friezes, decorative elements, furnishings, accessories and paintings, and used them to decorate and furnish the rooms of their home. The Renaissance came to life in the period pieces that include paintings like that of *Saint Justine*, perhaps by Giovanni Bellini, *St. John the Baptist* by Bernardino Zenale and the *Enthroned Madonna with Saints* by Giampietrino, as well as precious items of furniture. When the antique pieces were damaged, the brothers immediately replaced them, so no gaps marred the coherence and unity of the place.

Palazzo del Senato

The Senate Building overlooks the Navigli canals, at the junction between Via Senato and Via Sant'Andrea, and since 1872 it has housed the vast State Archive.

The palace was founded by St. Charles Borromeo in 1579 to house the Helvetic College; the façade is by Francesco Maria Richini (1629) and it is preceded by the bronze *Mère Ubu* sculpture by Mirò.

Villa Reale

The Royal Villa was built in 1790-1796 by Leopoldo Pollack, who studied with Piermarini, for Count Lodovico Barbiano di Belgioioso, and it is certainly Milan's masterpiece of neoclassicism. During the Napoleonic period, it was the residence of the Viceroy, Eugène de Beauharnais. This is the home of the Galleria d'Arte Moderna.

The part facing Via Palestro is preceded by an inner court, enclosed by porticoes that house a selection of sculptures from the early nineteenth century.

The façade has bas-reliefs and tall columns set against the piano nobile. The rear prospect is marvellous, cadenced by Corinthian pillars and columns, flanked by projecting wings and crowned with gables. The prospect is enhanced by a small garden, which was created at the same time as the villa and includes a lake flanked with lawns and groups of sculptures.

Galleria d'Arte Moderna

The Gallery of Modern Art is a museum complex that is part of the civic art collection circuit, including the Musei del Castello (ancient art) and CIMAC (contemporary art). In general, the gallery's collections are prevalently dedicated to nineteenth-century Italian painting. Nevertheless, the display path is the result of various donations of entire collections, whose integrity was safeguarded. Consequently, the visit also includes a nucleus of ancient paintings, Oriental objects and important twentieth-century works. Thus, apart from the chronological sequence of the ground floor rooms and those on the piano nobile, there are also the following nuclei: the dazzling Grassi collection (donated in 1956); the Vismara collection (1981) that includes paintings, etchings and ceramics by foreign artists (Picasso, Matisse, Dufy) as well as Italians (noteworthy paint-

ings by Morandi, De Pisis and Campigli); the important nucleus of works by Marino Marini, personally donated by the artist in 1973, including paintings, great sculptures and bronzes, all displayed in a fascinating layout. Apart from typical themes (Pomona's female figure, jugglers, knight and horse) there is a particularly significant series of portraits of famous twentieth-century figures.

The villa's piano nobile leads into the actual art gallery, which was initially dedicated to nineteenth-century Italian art. The various rooms follow a chronological path and, on the whole, they are dedicated to individual artists: Appiani, Piccio, Hayez and, further on, a group of wax sculptures by Medardo Rosso. The rooms in the left wing show the evolution of various mid-century Italian currents. The Scapigliati movement includes Tranquillo Cremona, Ranzoni, Faruffini; the Divisionists are repre-

Giovanni Segantini,
Angel of life, *1894.*
Galleria d'Arte
Moderna.

Tranquillo Cremona,
High-Life,
1877.
Galleria d'Arte
Moderna.

Vincent van Gogh,
Breton women
and children, *1888.*
Galleria d'Arte
Moderna.
The Grassi
Collection.

Giovanni Fattori,
Road that rises,
1870-1875.
Galleria d'Arte
Moderna.

*Giuseppe Pellizza
da Volpedo,*
Fourth Estate, *1901.
Galleria d'Arte
Moderna.*

sented by Previati and, chiefly, Segantini, whose splendid *Angel of Life* can be admired here. The path ends with the works of artists who also made a social commitment, like Morbelli and Pellizza da Volpedo, whose famous *Fourth Estate* is shown here.

An ornate staircase leads to the Grassi Collection. Here we find Oriental antiquities, several Italian and foreign paintings (by Stanzione, Longhi, Gerard Dou, Van Wittel, Van Goyen), and a lavish collection of paintings and etchings from the nineteenth-twentieth century. However, this is dedicated mainly to Italian and French painting of the 1800s, fully attuned with the nature of the

gallery, to which it acts as a prestigious complement.

The Grassi and Vismara collections have enriched the gallery by adding masterpieces of Divisionists, Macchiaioli, Scapigliatura, works by great artists like Giovanni Boldini and Giuseppe de Nittis, as well as a number of works by French artists rarely found in Italian museums: Corot, Millet, Boudin, Jongkind, Sisley, Gauguin, Manet, Van Gogh, Cezanne and Toulose-Lautrec.

PAC, or the Pavilion of Contemporary Art designed by Ignazio Gardella, is located to the right of Villa Reale, and it is Milan's most important location for temporary exhibits of contemporary artwork.

Palazzo Dugnani

Built at the end of the seventeenth century and remodelled in the late eighteenth century, the decorations of several of its halls have been preserved, including the two-storey Hall of Honour, with a wrought-iron balcony, which was frescoed by Giambattista Tiepolo in 1731.

The museum collections were established in 1947 when a group of film enthusiasts founded the Fondazione Cineteca Italiana, devoted to safeguarding and promoting the heritage of cinema.

Over the years, the museum also expanded its collection of equipment, books and instruments, which tell the story of cinema from its origin: as early as Galileo's time, scientists studied the problem of projecting moving images. Because of the importance of its collections, since 1948 the Fondazione Cineteca Italiana has been a member of the International Federation of Film Archives (IFFA/FIAF).

The Museo del Cinema, or Film Museum, was established in 1987, from an idea by Walter Alberti and Gianni Comencini. The collections are displayed in several rooms on the ground floor of Palazzo Dugnani, and rare films are screened in a small cinema room.

Palazzo Dugnani, late seventeeth century.

Giambattista Tiepolo, The Continence of Scipio, *1731. Palazzo Dugnani.*

Museo di Scienze Naturali

The Museum of Natural History is located in a large building constructed in the late nineteenth century. Modelled after the Romanesque style, it was designed by architect Giovanni Ceruti. The museum was founded in 1838 and expanded over the years to become one of the most important in Europe. The first floor is devoted to vertebrates: there are numerous dioramas, display cases, reconstructions and skeletons. The multifaceted itinerary on the ground floor features various specialised sections (mineralogy, biology, entomology, malacology). The sector devoted to palaeontology, with skeletons and other fossil remains, is fascinating. Inside the museum, the room reconstructing the Settala Museum is also interesting – more for historic reasons than scientific ones – as it offers a wide-ranging overview of interdisciplinary materials inspired by the concept of the *Wunderkammer*. Manfredo Settala established the collection in the early seventeenth century, and then part of it went to the Ambrosiana Gallery and disappeared into its storerooms.

The museum is set in a small but lovely park – the Public Gardens – dotted with footpaths, faux rocks, a small lake and numerous monuments. The area towards Corso Venezia, with even rows of trees around the museum, dates from the work done by Piermarini in 1770. The Planetarium is located to the right of the museum. This small domed building, designed by Piero Portaluppi (1930), conducts important educational activities in astronomy.

Museo di Scienze Naturali.

The Planetarium.

Skeleton of an Allosaurus fragilis, from the North American Jurassic. Museo di Scienze Naturali.

Corso Venezia

Palazzo Serbelloni – and before it, Palazzo Bovara, designed by the architect Soave – point to the advent of high society in Borgo di Porta Orientale, the segment of Porta Venezia stretching from the circle of the Navigli to the Bastioni. At the time, living in Borgo di Porta Orientale symbolized wealth and prestige. The first to astonish the Milanese was Gaetano Belloni, who built the majestic building later known as Palazzo Rocca Saporiti. Less prestigious buildings, in a neoclassical style, were constructed next to it. During the second half of the nineteenth century, Milan's bourgeoisie came to predominate in the city and, attracted by the work being done around the castle, it neglected this illustrious thoroughfare. It was not until the late nineteenth century that the most refined members of the bourgeoisie rediscovered the taste and atmosphere of Corso Venezia. The buildings that bear witness to this revival are Palazzo Chiesa, the two Bocconi buildings and Palazzo Castiglioni, which established the Art Nouveau style in Milan.

Palazzo Serbelloni,
Corso Venezia.

Palazzo Rocca
Saporiti,
Corso Venezia.

Palazzo Castiglioni,
Corso Venezia.

Art Nouveau in Milan

Art Nouveau became popular in Milan, as in the rest of Italy – Turin in particular – at the turn of the twentieth century. This new style was epitomized by architects Sebastiano Locati and Achille Manfredini, artists who were already successful with other eclectic works completed in the last decades of the nineteenth century. Marvellous examples of Art Nouveau buildings can be admired in the triangle between Corso Venezia, Via Vivaio and Corso Monforte. Giulio Ulisse Arata represents the end of the Art Nouveau period in Milan with two highly significant works: Casa Felisari and the three Berri-Meregalli buildings. The two houses on Via Mozart and Via Barozzi were built between 1910 and 1912. Both flaunt the clever use of stone and carved concrete, the architect's speciality and a hallmark of Art Nouveau architecture in general. With its rich decorations and intentionally asymmetrical elements on the façade, the house on Via Cappuccini (1911-1914) is a masterpiece.

Extremely widespread outside the Bastioni, Art Nouveau never gained entry to the historic district, which maintained its restrained Neo-Renaissance style for years. The only exceptions are the houses by Alfredo Campanini on Corso Monforte (1911) and Via Bellini (1904-1906). Located nearby are Casa Fidia and Casa Sola-Brusca. The latter is famous for the marble ear that once housed an intercom. Casa Galimberti, built by the Galimberti brothers – who built Palazzo Castiglioni – is on Via Malpighi. Casa Galimberti was built in 1902-1905 and was designed by Giovan Battista Bossi. The elegance and simplicity of the Art Nouveau style is also reflected in the splendid balconies of Casa Laugier, at the corner of Piazzale Baracca and Corso Magenta.

Casa Berri-
Meregalli,
Via Cappuccini.

Casa Berri-
Meregalli, detail
of the balcony,
Via Mozart.

Casa Galimberti,
Via Malpighi.

Casa Laugier,
Corso Magenta
at the corner of
Piazzale Baracca.

Marble ear, once the
intercom of casa
Sola-Brusca.

Stazione Centrale

Milan's main railway station was constructed between 1925 and 1931, but the plans by Ulisse Stecchini date from 1912. The station was built after World War I and clearly reflects a tendency towards a colossal style. Built in Aurisma stone, the station is distinguished by numerous sculptures, and it became the first major work of the Fascist regime.

The Pirelli Building

Designed by architect Gio Ponti and built between 1956 and 1961, it is 127 metres (417´) tall, making it one of world's tallest buildings in reinforced concrete.

The intention behind this innovative building is clearly revealed by the architect's words: "When circling around a mountain, one can see woods, waterfalls, a town, a stronghold, and so on. Likewise, what must appear as one circles this building is a landscape, with different scenes from its different viewpoints." This led to the concept of a lone tower surrounded by low buildings.

*Stazione Centrale,
exterior, 1925-1931.*

*Stazione Centrale,
interior galleries.*

*Gio Ponti, Pirelli
Building,
1956-1961.
The extensive
damage, caused
when a small plane*

*flew into the
building in 2002,
can be seen on the
upper floors.*

Museo della Permanente

Its headquarters are located in an elegant nineteenth-century building on Via Turati. The Società per le Belle Arti ed Esposizione Permanente was founded by a group of artists and intellectuals in order to disseminate and promote figurative art. The museum has its own collection, composed of approximately 100 pieces – sculptures, paintings and graphic works – that have come through donations and awards. Its main activity involves organizing temporary exhibits. Since July 1999, the 100 most important works from CIMAC, which is closed for restoration, have been housed here temporarily. These include works by artists such as Boccioni, Modigliani, De Chirico, Fontana and Kandinsky. These masterpieces represent the core collection of the Museo del Novecento, which will be set up in Palazzo dell'Arengario.

Umberto Boccioni, Unique forms of continuity in space, *1913.* CIMAC.

Amedeo Modigliani, Portrait of Paul Guillaume, *1916.* CIMAC.

Brera, the artists' district

Palazzo di Brera

A simple noble *palazzo*, its construction began in 1627 to a design by Francesco Maria Richini. Initially planned to house the Jesuit schools, in 1774 it was transformed by Marie Thérèse to *Palazzo delle Scienze* (the portal, added in that period, is the work of Giuseppe Piermarini). It is a typical institution of the Age of Enlightenment and included an astronomy observatory, a great library that was prevalently of a scientific nature, and teaching structures, including the academy of fine art. In the early nineteenth century, this was extended to include the first core of the art gallery or *Pinacoteca*, with Lombard, Veneto and Marches works brought by the Napoleonic requisitions.
To provide more space for the museum, the church of Santa Maria di Brera was demolished. Subsequently, the collection grew and was separated from the academy to become one of the most important museums in Europe. Numerous and prestigious additions created problems in terms of space and management, and these difficulties continue to penalize the exhibition itinerary today. This problem will be resolved in part by the "Grande Brera" project that envisages the extension of the gallery to Palazzo Citterio, whose transformation into a display is designed according to a project by the architects James Stirling and Michael Wilford.

Palazzo di Brera, an inner courtyard with two orders of arches.

Art Gallery

This is located on the upper floor of Palazzo di Brera, and can be reached by the staircase at the rear of the courtyard, an opus by Richini and a typical example of seventeenth-century Milanese architecture, with two orders of arcades. The Art Gallery's most famous group comprises Venetian paintings from the fifteenth to the eighteenth century, including masterpieces such as the *Adoration of the Magi* by Stefano Zevio and Jacopo Bellini's *Madonna with Child*. Visitors can also admire the famous masterpiece by Andrea Mantegna, the *Dead Christ*. Other great names include Giovanni Bellini, Vittore Carpaccio, Titian, Lorenzo Lotto, Giambattista Tiepolo, Piazzetta, Guardi and Canaletto. The Lombard section is also quite lavish, with works by Giovanni da Milano, Bonifacio Bembo, Vincenzo Foppa, Bernardino Luini, Bramante and Bramantino. Giacomo Ceruti's *Seated Errand Boy with Basket, Eggs and Poultry* is a life-sized painting, and the subject is

Andrea Mantegna,
Dead Christ,
1500 circa.
Pinacoteca
di Brera.

Gentile Bellini,
St. Mark Preaching
in a Square
in Alexandria,
1504-1507.
Pinacoteca di Brera.

Giacomo Ceruti,
known as
Pitocchetto, Seated
Errand Boy with
Basket, Eggs
and Poultry, *1735.*
Pinacoteca di Brera.

a poor, innocent child who nevertheless powerfully conveys his dignity and his character with his gaze. The boy, who has a large basket, represents that part of humanity who had few chances to be portrayed on canvas. Bergamo and Brescia's sixteenth century are well represented with works by Moretto, Savoldo, Romanino, Moroni, while there is no lack of examples from the Cremona School, including Vincenzo Campi's famous *Fruit Vendor.* The works by Cerano, Morazzone and Giulio Cesare Procaccini are from the seventeenth century, and there is no mistaking Caravaggio's intense masterpiece, *Supper at Emmaus.*

There are fewer works by painters from central Italy, but they are no less important: from Urbino there is the *Montefeltro Altarpiece* by Piero della Francesca, a magnificent example of the perspective construction of architectural space. Apart from works by Italian masters, there are several significant masterpieces by foreign artists such as El Greco, Rubens, Van Dyck and Rembrandt. The Italian nineteenth century opens with neoclassical works by Andrea Appiani. The numerous canvases by Hayez include the extremely romantic work *The Kiss.* The Divisionists are worthy of mention, with *Spring Pastures* by Giovanni Segantini and Pellizza da Volpedo's *Torrent.* Boccioni's *Self-portrait* is also an example of Divisionism.

Italian twentieth-century painting is noteworthy: the historical twentieth-century avant-garde is represented by the works of artists such as Severini, Sironi, Modigliani, De Pisis, Scipione, Mafai and Morandi.

Francesco Hayez,
The Kiss, *1859.*
Pinacoteca di Brera.

Santa Maria del Carmine

The Late Gothic construction of Santa Maria del Carmine was completed with materials from the demolished Visconti castle. The façade visible from the piazza dates from the late nineteenth century, while the interior retains its fifteenth-century Gothic appearance. The layout consists of a nave and two aisles set on pillars and the walls are decorated with countless seventeenth-century paintings; to the right of the presbytery, the Baroque Madonna del Carmine chapel is decorated with canvases by Camillo Procaccini.

In front of the church there is a statue by Igor Mitoraj. This Polish painter and sculptor came to Italy and travelled to Pietrasanta, where he discovered that the best material for his sculptures was marble rather than clay. In 1983 he opened a studio in Pietrasanta and now spends much of his time there.

The subject of his sculpture is the result of the artist's extensive evolution in his quest for truth: perhaps the fracture alludes to the mystery of history, which appears to us as fragments, illusions, and evocations. Several scholars and enthusiasts of Mitoraj maintain that the sculptor first constructs the entire form and then pares it down to only that part from which something pure and essential gleams.

Igor Mitoraj's bronze sculpture in Piazza del Carmine. In the background, the façade of Santa Maria del Carmine.

The streets of Brera

Via Brera is reached by going along the side of the church and passing in front of Palazzo Cusani, an eighteenth-century building by Giovanni Ruggeri that now houses military headquarters. This is heaven on earth for shopping aficionados, and it is the place that best expresses Milanese taste. Prestigious art galleries and artists' shops can be found along Via Brera. Bar Jamaica was the haunt of artists in the Fifties and Sixties, when Brera was the quintessential bohemian district.

Via Fiori Chiari is a tiny jewel of a street, with smart shops: it is difficult to believe that not long ago this was a working-class district. The old blocks of city housing are now luxury apartments. The taste for history and elegance can be sensed everywhere: there are numerous antiquarians and an antiques market is held every third Saturday of the month.

Via Fiori Chiari.

The streets of Brera come alive with countless outdoor cafés.

Palazzo Cusani faces out onto Via Brera.

San Marco

The church was founded in the mid-thirteenth century and originally looked out onto a canal. The various stages of its construction can be seen on the exterior: the transept juts from the apse and the rest of the building is Gothic; the right side, along Via Fatebenefratelli, shows a lively sequence of noble chapels (sixteenth-eighteenth century); and the Neo-Gothic façade has retained several fourteenth-century sculptures. The interior is prevalently Baroque in appearance. The chapels and altars are decorated with frescoes and canvases from the sixteenth to the eighteenth century, including works by Giovan Paolo Lomazzo, Giulio Cesare Procaccini and Palma the Younger, while a *Madonna with St Giovannino in Grisaille*, the work of an unknown painter inspired by Leonardo, can be seen at the third altar to the left. The presbytery has seventeenth-century furnishing and frescoes by Genovesino, as well as a large canvas by Cerano on the left wall. The right transept has retained its thirteenth-century structure and important remains of fourteenth-century frescoes: around and inside the apse chapels there are numerous reliefs and sculpted sarcophagi from the fourteenth century, including that of the Blessed Lanfranco Settala, founder of the church: This work by Giovanni di Balduccio portrays the monk in his chair. The left transept leads to the sacristy and the small museum, with remains of medieval frescoes, religious furnishings and paintings, including the splendid *Flight to Egypt* by Antonio Campi.

San Marco, façade.

Antonio Campi,
Flight to Egypt,
1577. San Marco,
museum.

Sant'Angelo,
façade .

Sant'Angelo

Sant'Angelo, built in the mid-sixteenth century, is a coherent example of Late Renaissance architecture and decoration in Lombardy. The façade, which has two orders and is dense with architectural elements and statues, was completed in the early 1600s. The interior comprises a single, spacious nave, with a barrel vault and side chapels. An arch separates the nave from the transept space and apse chapels. There are sumptuous decorations on the arches and vaults; the chapels boast of sixteenth and seventeenth-century canvases by artists such as Antonio Campi, Fiamminghini, Procaccini and Morazzone. The annexed Franciscan convent was reconstructed in 1940 by the architect Giovanni Muzio.

San Simpliciano

The basilica of San Simpliciano, erected by St. Ambrose in the fourth century, still has the appearance of an early Christian basilica, with the addition of a transept wing in the Romanesque period. The great portal is also Romanesque and it is one of the most historic parts of the façade, recomposed in the second half of the nineteenth century by Maciachini. The interior is quite charming, with an unusual combination of early Christian and Romanesque elements. At the sides of the presbytery there are two sixteenth-century organ stands with paintings by Aurelio Luini. In the apse there is a fresco by Bergognone (*Coronation of the Virgin*).

San Simpliciano, façade with Romanesque portal.

San Simpliciano, interior.

Santa Maria Incoronata

The church of Santa Maria Incoronata is the result of an original series of fifteenth-century architectural interventions, which have endowed it with a Late Gothic appearance. The façade with two cusps seems to evoke the flanking of twin churches, and this is indeed the case. The right side presents a sequence of jutting polygonal chapels, whereas the left side is part of the perimeter of the former Augustinian convent.

The interior has two aisles whose architectural lines are not totally similar, as the right-hand one was built a few years later (1460) and has handsome capitals. There are numerous sculpted fifteenth-century tablets, especially in the right-hand chapels. The first chapel to the left has a fresco by Ambrogio Bergognone (*Christ Interrogated*).

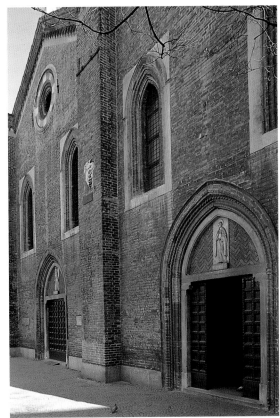

*Santa Maria
Incoronata,
fifteenth century,
façade.*

Cimitero Monumentale

The monumental cemetery, designed by Carlo Maciachini, was built between 1863 and 1866, and it is an exemplary model of the reinterpretation of historic architectural themes, inspired by mediaeval Lombard tradition. It was opened to the public on 1 January 1867 and was intended to replace Milan's old district cemeteries. It later became the graveyard for Milan's bourgeoisie. Today, its area of 200,000 square metres (nearly 50 acres) hosts monumental tombs, chapels and statues that illustrate the architecture and sculpture of the late nineteenth century. The long façade is set around a central octagon, the so-called "Famedio", from the Latin *Famae Aedes* (House of Fame), which holds the tombs of illustrious figures including Alessandro Manzoni, Carlo Cattaneo, Arturo Toscanini and Salvatore Quasimodo. Even a casual stroll reveals a number of admirable sections: from the Impressionism of Medardo Rosso to the Realism of Vincenzo Tela and Enrico Butti, the elegant symbolism of Bistolfi and Bazzaro, Art Nouveau, the Expressionism of Wildt, Giannino Castiglioni's "return to order" and the most recent expressions (Messina, Manzù, Cascella).

The richness of the monuments constitutes such an important artistic heritage that the cemetery can be considered a full-fledged museum: the management even organises exhibits and shows of worldwide interest.

Carlo Maciachini, Monumental Cemetery , 1866.

Detail of funerary monuments.

NON COLA MA VOLA
NON CADE MA S'ALZA

Around the Castle

Piazza Cordusio and Via Dante

The name of this piazza commemorates the "Cortis Ducis", the residence of the Longobard dukes: in fact, the piazza is located behind the Roman Imperial building. It emerged from the city planning scheme of the late nineteenth century, stretching from the Duomo to the Castle. Piazza Cordusio is the starting point for Via Dante, which was completed in 1890 and is lined with elegant buildings reminiscent of those along Parisian *boulevards*. The street has now been closed to traffic, making it ideal for a leisurely stroll from the Duomo towards the majestic Castello.

Piazza Cordusio seen from Via Dante.

Castello Sforzesco: the castle with the tower by Filarete.

Following pages
Castello Sforzesco, exterior.

Castello Sforzesco

The Castle is located in the lush Sempione Park, and it has lost much of its military character, enhancing its role as a stately home and cultural location. Its new appearance is the result of the restoration undertaken a century ago by Luca Beltrami. This work entailed demolishing the star-shaped system of bulwarks, recuperating the ducal court, reconstructing the battlements, roofs, walkways and part of the interior decoration, and constructing a new tower replacing Filarete's original, which collapsed in 1521. This operation restored the Castle as a monument testifying to the history of the city and as the prestigious home to a museum collection.

A visit of the Castello Sforzesco museums covers a single path through the various sections of the civic collections of ancient and decorative arts. The two basements dedicated to archaeology are an important adjunct.

The ground floor of the ducal court is devoted almost entirely to civic sculpture collections that include statues, reliefs and fragments, which span the fourth to sixteenth centuries and were obtained from Milanese buildings that no longer exist. The most historic works are in the first salons, including the head of the Empress Theodora, as well as various Longobard and Romanesque

Ravelin, fortified guardhouse of the Visconti period.

Castello Sforzesco, Parade Ground.

*Michelangelo
Buonarroti,*
Rondanini Pietà,
1564.

*Castello Sforzesco,
Sforzesco, Museum
of Ancient Art.*

Lorenzo Lotto,
Portrait of a young
man with a book,
1526. Castello
Sforzesco, Museum
of Ancient Art.

ornamental sculptures. Room VIII, located in the Falconiera tower, is the "Asse" room, frescoed by Leonardo da Vinci, who transformed the vault into an intricate pergola composed of the fronds of sixteen trees. Current decoration is mainly the result of retracing executed during Luca Beltrami's restoration: the monochrome fragments in the corner opposite the entrance are quite charming, with roots amidst the stones. The room hosts a permanent display of seventeenth-century Flemish and Dutch paintings that are part of the Belgiojoso collection.

There follows a group of rooms that preserve their fifteenth-century decoration and host sculptures of that era by Jacopino da Tradate, Amadeo, Mantegazza, Agostino di Duccio. There is a charming chapel, known as the Ducale, with Late Gothic frescoes, dated 1472, by a number of different artists guided by Bonifacio Bembo.

Room XIV is the home of the civic arms collection, with sixteenth-century weapons, numerous examples of lances and swords, and decorated firearms in precious materials. The last room is dedicated to sixteenth-century sculptures. Fragments of the monument to Gaston de Foix, an unfinished masterpiece by Bambaia and example of classic Lombard art, can be seen in the gardens. The *Rondanini Pietà* (1564), Michelangelo's final example of his dramatic talent, which he was unable to complete, has been installed in a special niche.

The first rooms on the piano nobile host furniture collections, with objects dating from the fifteenth to the late eighteenth century, with cabinetry masterpieces of various origins, like the Late Gothic *coretto di Torrechiara* (about 1460), the Passalacqua casket (1613) and the tallboy by Giuseppe Maggiolini. The frescoes include the important cycle of *Griselda Stories*, detached from the walls of Roccabianca castle, a work by an unknown master of the mid-fifteenth century.

The Civica Pinacoteca, or city picture gallery, is arranged in the rooms that were once the Duke's private apartments. Room XX has fifteenth-century Lombard school works (Benedetto Bembo) as well as paintings from the Venetian school (Giovanni Bellini, Crivelli, Mantegna) and some Tuscans (Sano di Pietro, Filippo Lippi). The next room displays works by Vincenzo Foppa, Bergognone, Bramantino, Cesare da Sesto and several Leonardesque works. There are also paintings by masters from Bergamo and Brescia, like Moretto, Romanino, Moroni.

Room XXV displays prestigious portraits by Giovanni Bellini, Lotto, Correggio, Bronzino, Tintoretto, Moroni, Titian, Van Dyck, Fra Galgario, Ceruti, Nattier and Greuze.

The last room is dedicated to the comparison between

Antonio Allegri called Correggio, Madonna with Child and St. Giovannino, *1514-1517. Castello Sforzesco, Museum of Ancient Art.*

Andrea Mantegna Madonna in glory amidst saints and angels *(Trivulzio* *Altarpiece), 1497. Castello Sforzesco, Museum of Ancient Art.*

various schools of Baroque painting. To the left there are works by the Lombards (Cerano, Morazzone, Daniele Crespi, Francesco Cairo), while those on the right are Venetian, Genoese and Neapolitan works. At the back of the room, there are eighteenth-century canvases, including a group of landscapes by Magnasco, two sketches by Giambattista Tiepolo and various works by Sebastiano Ricci and Francesco Guardi.

The Rocchetta's two upper floors house the city's collections of decorative arts. This extensive complex has significant examples of artistic production using a wide range of techniques.

There is a particularly noteworthy and complete panorama of Italian majolica produced from the fifteenth to the eighteenth century. A mezzanine hosts a rotating display of several examples of historic costume. The porcelain showcases are followed by the collections of religious and secular jewellery. Apart from a group of bronzes, the room is completed by a small but important collection of scientific instruments.

The museum of historical musical instruments begins on the first floor of the Rocchetta. The lavish collection is arranged as groups of similar instruments: the series of harpsichords, spinets and pianos is quite extraordinary, with decorated examples and strange shapes. Some of the more antique instruments are displayed in the "Balla" salon, the biggest in the castle, which was used by the Sforza for entertaining. It now exhibits the twelve tapestries on the months of the year, the *Arazzi Trivulzio*, woven in Vigevano between 1504 and 1509 to drawings by Bramantino. Each scene depicts the allegory for that month, with farm tasks and the signs of the zodiac.

The Rocchetta's basement completes the museum itinerary. There is a fascinating room that houses the materials of the Golasecca civilization, from the Late Bronze Age to the Roman invasion. The Egyptian section features painted sarcophagi, statues, vases and other items. The Loggia Ducale accesses the basement called "Ritrovare Milano" [rediscovering Milan]. The two large rooms host a lavish Roman epigraphic museum with stones, epigraphs and stele brought from excavations in the city, and there is also a group of mediaeval and Renaissance sculptures.

Leonardo da Vinci, decoration with intertwined foliage, 1498. Castello Sforzesco, Asse room, vault.

Donato Bramante and Bramantino, Argo, 1493, detached fresco. Castello Sforzesco, Treasure room.

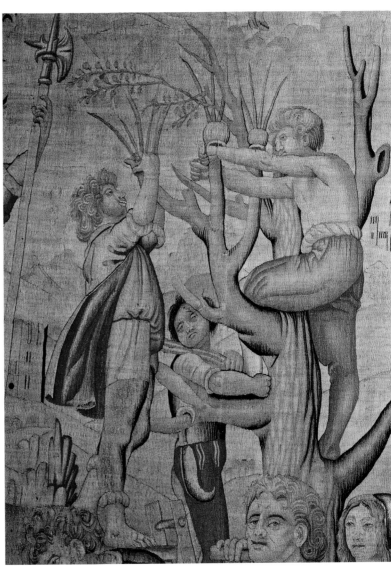

Strehler and his Piccolo Teatro

The date is 14 May 1947: the curtain rises on the first performance of this brand-new theatre, the Piccolo Teatro of Milan. This enchanting place was the result of a friendship. In fact, the Via Rovello theatre was born from the friendship between two boys who had met many years earlier.

One was Paolo Grassi from Puglia and the other was Giorgio Strehler who came from Trieste. At the beginning of its history the "Piccolo" was "piccolo" – or small – in all senses, but great performances were staged here: *Arlecchino, servitore di due padroni* [*Harlequin, servant of two masters*] was certainly the longest-running comedy. Through the nine productions, we can observe the thrilling, unique experience of Strehler's theatre. The first production was in the summer of 1947: the scenery was simple, the costumes were inspired by tradition and the actors wore stiff, painful masks. Harlequin was different each time: sometimes set in an Italian square, outdoors with wagons carrying a troupe of wandering players who performed Goldoni's text and represented a truly Italian theatrical tradition. Goldoni's works yielded famous performances like *Le Baruffe chiozzotte* [*Quarrels in Chioggia*], *Il campiello* [*The Venetian Square*], as well as Anton Chekhov's *Cherry Garden*, Goethe's masterpiece *Faust*, Brecht's *Threepenny Opera* and *Life of Galileo*, and Shakespeare's *King Lear*, *The Tempest*, *Henry VI*, and *Richard III*. In the Sixties, Grassi and Strehler requested a new location. The area between Foro Bonaparte and Via Rivoli and Via Tivoli was identified and the nineteenth-century Teatro Fossati located here was restored and renamed "Teatro Studio". The Nuovo Piccolo Teatro was built here, designed by Marco Zanuso. This was the venue for Strehler's last masterpiece, Mozart's *Così fan tutte*: the director died in December 1997, leaving great emptiness in the hearts of the people of Milan and in the history of European theatre. Today, the Piccolo Teatro is a complex of three auditoriums: the historic Via Rovello site, the Teatro Studio, and the Nuovo Piccolo Teatro. The latter has a state-of-art stage and seats 999 spectators, and the playhouse stages theatre, music, ballet, jazz, cinema. Milan was thus the first city in Italy to offer a full-fledged multimedia theatre complex.

Giorgio Strehler (1921-1997) during rehearsals (photos by Luigi Ciminago).

The Nuovo Piccolo Teatro was designed by Marco Zanuso.

A scene from Così fan tutte, *by W.A. Mozart, directed by G. Strehler, sets by E. Frigerio.*

Parco Sempione

The park is located between the Sforza fortress and Corso Sempione, to which it owes its name. Parco Sempione is Milan's second largest public park and covers 47 hectares, making it the biggest in the city centre. It was created between 1890 and 1893 by the architect Emilio Alemagna on the site of the "Barcho", which in the 1400s was the largest of the ducal gardens. The English-style park has a vast central lawn, framed by avenues and thickets, and then it extends northwards for its entire length, creating a splendid play of perspectives between the Castle and the Arco della Pace [Arch of Peace], set respectively at either end. Halfway between the two monuments, there is a small lake that stretches laterally into two basins, one of which is bridged by the *Ponte della Sirenetta*, brought here from its original position on the Navigli canal network, when the canals were covered. It is decorated by four cast-iron mermaids that the Milanese call the "sorelle Ghisini" or cast-iron sisters. De Chirico's *Fontana metafisica* or *Bagni misteriosi* is located at the centre of the park, and there are playing fields set close to the hill of Mount Tordo, which is the site of the monument to Napoleon III by Francesco Barzaghi. There is also a small district library.

View of Parco Sempione, towards the Castello Sforzesco.

Parco Sempione, Sirenetta *bridge.*

City Aquarium

Just outside the gates around the central park area is the Arena, or Stadio Civico, a neoclassical structure built by Luigi Canonica in 1806 and used for sports events of various kinds. The nearby Art Nouveau building hosts the city aquarium [Acquario Civico] founded in 1906, one of the oldest in the world. The Aquarium has thirty-six tanks with about 100 species of aquatic organisms. Visitors can see various Mediterranean habitats such as the coastal zones and sandy shoreline. There is a fascinating and meticulous reconstruction of the amber waters of the Amazon, archer fish hunting in a saltwater environment, and a section of coral barrier typical of tropical seas. At the end of the visit there is an enormous terrarium, with amphibians concealed by the vegetation. Each tank has its own luminous panel that offers information on the aquatic environment and organisms. In the rear garden, a number of aquatic environments have been created to illustrate typical Po Valley environments.

Triennale and Torre Branca

Palazzo dell'Arte, the home of Milan's Triennial exhibition, is located at the opposite end of the park to the Aquarium, and it is flanked by the Parco tower – formerly known as the Torre Littoria (now Torre Branca) – a construction in steel pipe that is 109 metres (354´) high and was built in 1932, designed by Cesare Chiodi, Gio Ponti and Ettore Ferrari. Recently it was refurbished and the tower now houses a panoramic lift that allows visitors to enjoy the spectacular view over the city.

City Aquarium,
1906.

Torre Branca,
1932.

The entrance to
Palazzo dell'Arte,
home of the Milan
Triennial.

Piazza Cadorna

After the refurbishment commissioned by the municipal council and entrusted to Gae Aulenti, this formerly grey and chaotic thoroughfare was transformed into a colourful, harmonious space, the perfect place for a stroll. Like all piazzas, it naturally has a statue: *Needle, thread and knot*, a sculpture by Claes Oldenburg and Coosje van Bruggen, pays homage to the industrious citizens of Milan. This 18-metre (58.5´) work was created in satin-finish stainless steel and fibreglass, and is the symbol of this new Piazza Cadorna. The statue is a fitting element for the junction of streets: the needle is at the centre of the piazza and its eye is aligned with the castle tower; the 80 metres (260´) of "thread in red, yellow and green – the colours of the three underground transport lines – spiral around it as far as road level, and emerge in a fountain as a knot with a diameter of three metres (9.75´), with tips extending for six metres (19.5´).

This needle with knotted thread, ready to use, symbolizes industrious Milan, the city that "sews" haute-couture creations, but also "stitches" relationships with different cultures and ethnic groups.

Santa Maria delle Grazie

The Dominican convent is Milan's most prestigious fifteenth-century architectural and decorative complex.

Two separate building phases can be identified: the front of the church was built to a design by Guiniforte Solari, starting in 1466, and it still expresses its deep Gothic heritage. It has a very low, gabled façade, whereas the interior has a nave and two aisles, a cross vault with groin ribs and a series of square side chapels. In about 1490, although he was not yet duke of the city Ludovico il Moro became lord of Milan and began to renovate the church, starting with the construction of the portal whose lunette contained a mural painting by Da Vinci, which has since been lost, depicting the Virgin with Ludovico and Beatrice. He subsequently began work on the new tribune.

The design of the new section was entrusted to Bramante. The new tribune was given a central plan, inspired by the model used for Roman buildings that fasci-

Claes Oldenburg,
Coosje van Bruggen,
Needle, thread and
knot, *2000.*
Piazza Cadorna.

Santa Maria delle
Grazie, façade.
The portal is by
Donato Bramante.

Donato Bramante,
Santa Maria
delle Grazie, apse,
1492.

nated Renaissance architects, who linked precise ideological, symbolic and moral meanings to it. The cupola area has a neighbouring room: this layout is clearly visible in the old sacristy and Brunelleschi's Pazzi chapel, arranged over the two connected rectangles. This was a typical Tuscan model, brought to Lombardy by Michelozzo when he worked on the Portinari chapel in the church of Sant'Eustorgio.

However, the solution chosen for the exterior, an arcade enclosing the volume, reflects pure Lombard tradition. This differed from the Tuscan model, which preferred a cupola with an unencumbered calotte. The tribune is accessed via a courtyard and large staircase: the great arches support the dome, which features sgraffito decoration, as do the pendentives. Other sgraffito work deco-

rates the apse vault and the walls above the inlaid choir. The best observation point for the tribune is Bramante's chiostrino, or small cloister. The portals towards the church and the sacristy have monochrome frescoed lunettes by Bramantino.

The old sacristy is a great apsidal room. There are painted wooden balconies along the walls and the ceiling is decorated with Leonardo-style motifs.

Santa Maria delle Grazie, the tiburium in the large cloister.

Santa Maria delle Grazie, interior, the part done by Solari: a view of the nave looking down towards the tribune, set on longitudinal ogival arches on columns.

Donato Bramante, apse vault, 1492.

Following pages
Leonardo da Vinci,
Last Supper,
1494-1498.
Santa Maria delle Grazie, refectory.

The Last Supper

Leonardo painted the Last Supper on the walls of the Santa Maria delle Grazie refectory between 1494 and 1498, commissioned by Ludovico il Moro. The Last Supper is Leonardo's art at its peak: in this work, he sublimely expressed the "commotion of the spirit". In other words, he depicted what occurs in the mind and soul of the figures by capturing their physical reactions in gestures, posture and facial expressions. The most striking moment comes when Christ utters the words "One of you will betray me", and they are heard by the apostles, triggering a series of dramatic reactions.

The painting began to deteriorate in 1517 and became almost invisible in the mid-sixteenth century. The work was evidently restored quite early, as sections gradually flaked away due to the humidity of the room and the walls. The left side shows traces of old retouching to repair the flaking paint: red and black stucco, which probably date back to the 1600s or even the mid-1500s. The first documented intervention was by Michelangelo Bellotti in 1726. Subsequently, there were countless futile attempts to save the work. In the early twentieth century, when it was thought that the Last Supper was lost forever, Luigi Cavenaghi intervened by cleaning and securing the pictorial surface. In 1924, the borders, at that time reduced to mere scraps of paint, were fixed with greyish stucco. The 1943 bombings led to the collapse of the east wall and the entire vault, but not the wall with the painting, which had been protected by sandbags. The subsequent reconstruction produced extensive dampness, and during the 1947 inspection the Last Supper looked completely whitewashed. It was consolidated in 1949 and al-

though the ancient touch-ups of the 1700-1800s were not removed, the brilliant results of this work restored the masterpiece's former splendour.

The most recent restoration began in 1977 to repair the peeling of small sections of paint from the surface. Between 1978 and 1983, the four lunettes above the group of Apostles on the right were completely cleaned. From 1985 to 1991, various research institutes were appointed to conduct research and analysis: the restoration of the painting was then resumed more intensively and the intervention method was modified, integrating missing sections of the work using the watercolour "rigatino" technique.

Leonardo da Vinci,
Last Supper,
1494-1498, detail.
Santa Maria delle
Grazie, refectory.

Donato
Montorfano,
Crucifixion, *1495.*
Santa Maria delle
Grazie, refectory.

Santa Maria at San Satiro

The church consists of two blocks: the San Satiro or Pietà chapel, a Carolingian structure (ninth century) with an elegant fifteenth-century façade is next to the ancient bell tower, erected in the tenth century, and along the side is Bramante's church, or "Santa Maria presso San Satiro".
The façade was completed in the last century. The interior is the work of Bramante (1478): using pioneering perspective solutions, Bramante transformed a small space into a vast basilica, thanks to a barrel vault in the nave, a wide transept with pillars and, to the spectacular faux presbytery stratagem: a narrow niche decorated with a terracotta relief that simulates a deep choir. At the rear of the left arm of the transept we enter the Pietà chapel, with its Greek-cross plan. Built in the ninth century, and partly altered in the fifteenth century. The altar holds the Pietà, a terracotta group by Agostino de' Fondulis, dating back to 1483. The top of the right aisle leads to the baptistery, an octagonal room in two orders, designed by Bramante and decorated with terracotta friezes by de' Fondulis.

San Sebastiano

It was built by Saint Charles at the time of the 1576 plague. The main cylindrical body of the building, to which the presbytery was added at the end of the sixteenth century, is by architect Pellegrino Tibaldi. An example of Milanese Late Renaissance architecture, the church rigorously applies the classical formal code, based on the Ionic style. The interiors of the side chapels are decorated with canvases by various Lombard artists of the late seventeenth century.

San Sepolcro

The nineteenth-century façade pays homage to the original Romanesque style. The interior was restored in the seventeenth century by Francesco Maria Richini and houses two groups of sixteenth-century terracotta statues. The crypt, which is a remnant of the Romanesque construction (eleventh century), contains another clay sculpture, the *Deposition*, from the circle of Agostino de' Fondulis.

Bramante, false choir in Santa Maria at San Satiro.

San Sebastiano, the tiburium by Pellegrino Tibaldi.

San Sepolcro, façade.

Palazzo Borromeo

Significant traces remain of the building's fifteenth-century construction, such as the ogival portal in the façade, surmounted by the Borromeo family's heraldic dromedary. The courtyard leads to a room decorated with a fresco cycle dating back to the mid-fifteenth century, the work of an anonymous Late Gothic artist.

Santa Maria a Podone

Located opposite Palazzo Borromeo, it part of the area that belongs to the Borromeo family. Preceded by a seventeenth-century bronze statue of Saint Charles, the church retains some of its Late Gothic structure, as part of the renovation work done by Fabio Mangone in the early 1600s.

Maestro dei Giochi Borromeo, active around the mid-fifteenth century, The Ball Game. *Palazzo Borromeo.*

Santa Maria a Podone, façade.

The entrance to the Pinacoteca or Ambrosiana Picture Gallery.

The Ambrosiana

This austere building, part of which dates from the seventeenth-century, houses Milan's oldest and most distinguished cultural institution. In the early 1600s, Cardinal Federico Borromeo, decided to endow the city with a centre for literary and religious studies open to the public, and he thus collected a large number of manuscripts and books. The library was inaugurated in 1609 and the books were made available to everyone. In 1618 Cardinal Federico completed the operation by opening his own collection of paintings to the public and linking an Academy of Fine Arts to the picture gallery. Even after Borromeo's death in 1631, the Ambrosiana's educational and cultural activity was very lively: the site was repeatedly extended, incorporating previous buildings, and both the library and the picture gallery benefited from an ongoing series of acquisitions and additions. The entire building was renovated in 1993.

The Ambrosiana library is one of the most important in the world, with more than 35,000 manuscripts and 2,500 *incunabola* (books printed before the year 1500). Its most valuable asset is the collection of drawings by Leonardo da Vinci, including the monumental *Atlantic Codex*. It also has several priceless drawings, including a notebook of sketches by Rubens, the *Resta Codex* anthology, numerous folios by Lombard Renaissance and seventeenth-century artists. The picture gallery revolves around Federico Borromeo's core collection. In addition to paintings there are also displays of sculptures, precious metal artefacts, miniatures and objets d'art. There is a rich Renaissance section with an important series by Bramantino and Bernardino Luini, and a group of Leonardesque works that form the backdrop to Leonardo's masterpiece, *The Portrait of a Musician*.

Following pages
Caravaggio, Basket
of Fruit, *1596.*
Ambrosiana
Picture Gallery.

The famous work by Caravaggio, *The Basket of Fruit*, is an incomparable example of the still-life genre which also includes works by Evaristo Baschenis and Fede Galizia. The Venetian paintings include numerous works by Titian, Jacopo da Bassano's *Rest on the Flight into Egypt*, and the *Portrait of a Gentleman* by Giovan Battista Moroni.

There are many other masterpieces, such as the *Virgin with the Baldachin* by Botticelli, a *Virgin* by Pinturicchio and, above all, Raphael's exquisite cartoon for the *School of Athens*.

Bartolomeo Suardi, known as Bramantino, Nativity, *fifteenth-sixteenth century. Ambrosiana Picture Gallery.*

Leonardo da Vinci, Portrait of a Musician, *1485. Ambrosiana Picture Gallery.*

Bruegel il Vecchio, Vase of flowers with jewel and coin, *1606. Ambrosiana Picture Gallery.*

*San Maurizio,
façade.*

Bernardino Luini,
Christ at the
Column, *1630.
San Maurizio,
chapel of Santa
Caterina.*

San Maurizio

The tall austere façade of the church of San Maurizio be-
lies the sumptuous beauty of the Renaissance church in
the ancient Maggiore monastery, once the city's most
important convent.

Demolitions and renovation work done in the past have
not altered the appearance of San Maurizio, whose sixteenth-century decoration and structure has been preserved intact.

The building, attributed to Gian Giacomo Dolcebuono,
dates back to 1503. A wall divides the interior into two
halls, one for the congregation and the other for masses.
The sides are cadenced by a series of Serlian loggias
that frame the side chapels. The available spaces are
painted, mainly by Bernardino Luini and his school
(1522-1529). The partition, decorated by Luini with
beautiful figures of female saints is particularly interesting. The decoration continues in the rear room, which
is accessed through the left-hand chapels. On the partition are *Stories of the Passion of Christ*, again by
Bernardino Luini, who also painted some of the landscapes that decorate the side chapels.

The frescoes in the lunettes and the tondoes with busts
of female saints are the work of Giovanni Antonio
Boltraffio and Bernardino Zenale. The organ, with a
painted structure, is a masterpiece by Giovan Giacomo
Antegnati (1554).

Ansperto Tower and remains of the Late Roman walls.

Rhyton (vase for ritual libations) with a female head, 420-400 B.C. Museo Archeologico.

Archaeological Museum

The Museum is located in the rooms of the former Maggiore monastery, along Corso Magenta. The exhibition site was created in 1965 to link the entrance cloister and the back garden, with its Roman walls and towers, and it is used as a venue for temporary exhibitions and teaching activities. At the centre of the colonnaded courtyard is the *Masso di Borno*, a sacred stone decorated with the rock carvings typical of Val Camonica (second-third millennium BC). Roman remains are exhibited on the ground floor. There is a noteworthy group of portraits, fragments of sculptures including a head of Zeus (second century AD), a painted plinth and various priceless remains from the Imperial Age. Masterpieces include the *Diatreta Cup*, a block of glass elegantly covered in mesh, and the *Parabiago Patera*, a large embossed silver disc with scenes linked to the cult of Cybele. A masterpiece of the Late Roman goldsmith's art, the Patera is probably the work of the same workshop that made the Saint Nazarius *capsella* (reliquary), now in the Cathedral Treasury. The Greek and Etruscan sections are in the basement. In the rear garden there are various sculptural remains as well as the Ansperto Tower, a twenty-sided structure erected at the time of the Emperor Maximianus and later integrated into the mediaeval walls. Another Roman tower, originally linked to the Circus and built in the eighth century, serves as the belfry for San Maurizio.

Patera with Cybele and Attis, late fourth century. Museo Archeologico.

From Sant'Ambrogio to the Navigli Canals

Sant'Ambrogio

This large church is a classic example of Romanesque architecture, but with substantial remains of previous phases. It is located in an area characterised by strong historical traces, such as the "Pusterla di Sant'Ambrogio", a thirteenth-century city gate with fourteenth-century statues, the Roman Corinthian column known as the "Colonna del Diavolo" or Devil's Column and the Temple of Victory, a monument erected by Giovanni Muzio in 1930. Founded by Saint Ambrose in the fourth century, the basilica was built over the site of an ancient cemetery and was dedicated to the martyrs. Between the eighth and ninth century, the church became a Benedictine abbey and underwent its first transformations and additions. The church was subjected to further building work between the eleventh and twelfth centuries, the period when the complex acquired its present-day aspect. Further alterations were completed

Sant'Ambrogio,
the quadriporticus
and the interior.

*Sant'Ambrogio,
front of the
gold-laminated
altar with scenes
of the Life of Christ.*

during the Sforza era (fifteenth century) and to the Borromeo period (sixteenth-seventeenth century). The basilica is preceded by a characteristic Romanesque quadriporticus on pillars. Various marble remains and traces of frescoes can be seen under the arches. The gabled façade presents a large loggia with five arches of decreasing height, illuminating the interior.

The larger bell tower dates from the twelfth century, whereas the other one is a ninth-century relic.

The interior structure is frequently imitated in large Lombard Romanesque buildings. The length of the nave and two aisles, without a transept and with an octagonal tiburium, is cadenced by a series of four cross-vaulted

bays, supported by large clustered piers, each of which includes two smaller arches and the women's gallery loggias. The presbytery is closed by a semicircular apse. Along the left of the nave is the Romanesque pulpit that acts as a base for the sarcophagus of Stilico. The presbytery has a remarkable canopied ciborium, with splendid tenth-century stucco scenes, supported by four porphyry columns. Beneath it is the altar, a superb example of the Carolingian goldsmith's art by Vuolvinio (835). The four sides are finished in gold and silver leaf, with scenes from the Gospel and from the life of Saint Ambrose. The presbytery has retained its Early Christian structure. The apse basin contains a mosaic, *Christ*

in Glory and Stories of Saint Ambrose, which has been reassembled on a number of occasions with eighth and twelfth-century fragments. The crypt houses the modern urn with the bodies of Saints Ambrose, Gervasius and Protasius. The last chapel on the right leads to the San Vittore in Ciel d'Oro sacellum. Located at the end of the right-hand nave is the entrance to the "Canonica" portico, designed by Bramante in 1492 and the Sigismondo oratory is across from it.

Illuminated manuscripts, church ornaments and precious metal artefacts are located in the charming "Capitolino", whilst other enchanting works of art pertaining to the basilica are now in the Diocesan Museum.

San Vittore al Corpo

Built on the ruins of the Roman imperial mausoleum and completely renovated in the sixteenth century. Though the façade is simple, the composite interior is quite complex. The construction has a cruciform plan with a nave and two aisles, a large dome built above the transept with apse wings, a deep presbytery and elevated side chapels. The barrel vault of the nave, the rich stuccowork and frescoes create a stately aura characteristic of the Counter Reformation. The choir is the most precious element.

Science and Technology Museum

The Science and Technology Museum, named after Leonardo da Vinci is located in the ancient monastery of San Vittore, whose interior layout can still be perceived. This vast museum is the only one of its kind in Italy, and it traces the history of technological progress in various industrial and manufacturing sectors, using original items for educational reconstructions. There is an interesting railway pavilion with a charming Art Nouveau station, which features twenty locomotives and railway carriages, wheras the naval building, has enormous model ships. On the top floor, there are numerous aeroplanes of great historical importance. The science gardens surround the building and cover approximately 3,000 square metres, with several scientific itineraries and interactive machines for the use of visitors.

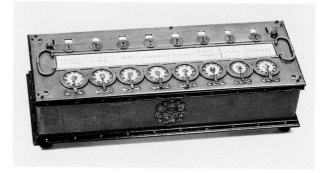

*San Vittore
al Corpo, façade.*

*Model of the beating
wing, reconstruction
from a drawing
by Leonardo da
Vinci. Science
and Technology
Museum.*

*The calculator
developed by Blaise
Pascal. Science
and Technology
Museum.*

Leonardo's Horse

Since September 1999, Milan has had a new monument: a gigantic bronze horse inspired by Leonardo's drawings.

The genius conceived the construction of the largest ever equestrian statue, an enterprise that combined art and technology. During his seventeen-year stay in Milan, Leonardo only managed to prepare a large clay model, which the French used as a crossbow target during the occupation of the city. Five hundred years later, in 1977, an American airline pilot was fascinated by the idea of making the horse that Leonardo had only seen in his mind. Dent's intention was to give it to the city of Milan, in gratitude for the Italian Renaissance, which gave so much to the entire world.

A foundation was set up to raise the extensive funds that were required. However, the main problem was that very little remained of Leonardo's original idea. Consequently, Dent established a scientific committee of Leonardo experts and had a model of the horse made. Finally, in 1999, under the guidance of the sculptress Nina Akamu, the horse was cast in small segments that were then assembled. In September of that year, the horse was taken to the San Siro Hippodrome in Milan, where it can now be admired in all its powerful beauty.

The bronze horse, inspired by Leonardo da Vinci, dominates the entrance to the San Siro hippodrome.

Columns and Basilica of San Lorenzo

The colonnade consists of sixteen fluted columns from the second-third century and it distinguishes the wide space opening out in front of the basilica of San Lorenzo, between Via del Carrobbio and Porta Ticinese. This is one of the surviving breaches in the thirteenth-century walls, although they were rebuilt in 1865 by Camillo Boito.

The columns were installed in front of the basilica in the fourth century as the façade of a quadriporticus whose entrance arch rises above the trabeation. The colonnade is Milan's most impressive archaeological relic.

Built between the fourth and fifth centuries as a Palatine basilica, it retains many parts of the original Early Christian central plan layout. The best point from which to view the complex is Piazza Vetra at its rear. Here, it is possible to recognize the early-Christian multilobed structure, comprising four exedras with bell towers at the intersections, surmounted by the sixteenth-century octagonal dome.

On the left are San Sisto, Sant'Ippolito and Sant'Aquilino chapels (fourth-fifth century); the latter is the largest. The interior confirms the solemnity of imperial art. Four large exedras with calottes support the dome, whereas groups of columns and pillars support the women's gallery

San Lorenzo, façade.

San Lorenzo, view from Piazza della Vetra.

Early Christian mosaic depicting Christ in the College of the Apostles. *San Lorenzo, Sant'Aquilino chapel.*

loggia and form a diaphragm between the ring-shaped ambulatory and the large central space. Romanesque interventions on the structure and the sixteenth-century reconstruction of the dome are visible. The walls are covered with decorations of various eras, with remains of frescoes from the twelfth to the seventeenth century. On the right is the entrance to the Sant'Aquilino chapel, built as an imperial mausoleum and enriched by a small loggia. Visitors enter via the barrel-vaulted atrium and a splendid Roman portal then leads into the chapel itself, which is traditionally thought to have been commissioned by Galla Placidia in about 380 AD.

San Paolo Converso

It was built in the mid-sixteenth century as the convent church of the monastery of the Angelical sisters. The façade was designed by Cerano and features robust statues and projecting architectural elements. The deconsecrated interior, which is difficult to access, is divided into two rooms by a partition. The vault was frescoed by the Campi brothers (1586-1589).

Santa Maria dei Miracoli at San Celso

The sanctuary, dedicated to Our Lady of Miracles, was begun in 1490 by Gian Giacomo Dolcebuono. The oldest part is the wide apse, surmounted by the polygonal tiburium, which was completed by Amadeo. The main entrance is preceded by a quadriporticus on pillars, the work of Cesare Cesariano (1513). The rear comprises the façade, which was built by Martino Bassi to a design by Galeazzo Alessi (1572) and is decorated with statues, herms and basreliefs – a veritable anthology of late-sixteenth-century Milanese sculpture. From a structural standpoint, the church has a nave and two aisles, a large dome and a wide ambulatory. There are numerous works of art on the altars in the shallow chapels. In addition to the sixteenth-century frescoes and altarpieces, noteworthy works include *Adoration of the Child* by Bergognone, *Baptism of Christ* by Gaudenzio Ferrari, *Fall of Saint Paul* by Moretto and *Saint Jerome* by Callisto Piazza. The right hand transept door leads to San Celso, founded by St. Ambrose and rebuilt in the Romanesque style in the eleventh century.

Columns of San Lorenzo, second-third century.

San Paolo Converso, façade.

San Celso, façade, eleventh century.

Sant'Eustorgio

A lovely clearing in the Park of the Basilicas links this church to the basilica of San Lorenzo. Its foundation dates back to the cult of the Magi, whose relics were allegedly brought to Milan in the early fourth century by Bishop Eustorgius. Part of the present-day building dates back to the eleventh century. It was renovated at the end of the following century, after Barbarossa destroyed part of it in 1162, when he stole the Magi relics and took them to Cologne. The various building phases are visible from the exterior. The façade shows extensive restoration work, whereas the right side is intact and has a vibrant series of constructions. The first three chapels are followed by the gabled Gothic Visconti chapels. The chapel that serves as the transept is older. The apse is a remnant of the eleventh-century building. Behind the apse stands the Portinari chapel, built between 1462 and 1468 at the behest of Pigello Portinari, a Florentine banker and representative in Milan during the time of the Sforza dynasty. Frescoed by Vincenzo Foppa between 1455 and 1468 (it is the only unfinished cycle by Foppa), the Portinari chapel takes Filippo Brunelleschi as its architectural point of reference (in particular the old sacristy in the church of San Lorenzo, in Florence), but it was also inspired to a great extent by the Lombard Romanesque-Gothic style. Recent studies have attributed it to Guiniforte Solari, who was the Sforza family's leading architect at the time. The restoration of the frescoes has removed the lime wash (applied after the 1630 plague) that had never been eliminated entirely, even after work undertaken in the 1920s, when fixatives were added. Humidity, nineteenth-century repainting and highly unskilled interventions jeopardized this masterpiece of the Lombard Renaissance. Nevertheless, the chapel can now be seen in all its exceptional beauty. The vault is painted with a motif of scales in bright colours. Along the base of the drum, the circle of dancing angels in painted terracotta relief has re-emerged. Beneath the arches, the marvellous cycle frescoed by Foppa and devoted to St. Peter Martyr has resurfaced with its rich hues, architectural perspectives and the inclusion of a landscape that marks the onset of naturalism. The oldest clock in Milan was mounted on the high, austere bell tower in the early fourteenth century.

*Sant'Eustorgio,
façade overlooking
the square by the
same name.*

*Sant'Eustorgio,
the south side with
fifteenth-century
chapels.*

*Sant'Eustorgio,
Portinari chapel,
detail of the
frescoes depicting
the* Miracle
of the Cloud.

Museo Diocesano

The Diocesan Museum is charmingly framed by the Cloisters of Sant'Eustorgio. The collection in the Diocesan Museum includes approximately 320 works, subdivided into ten basic sections.

Many works from the collections of the Milanese archbishops have come to the museum from the archiepiscopal picture gallery, thus revealing the different cultural orientations of Ambrose's successors to the bishopric. Of these, the museum houses part of the Monti, Visconti and Pozzobonelli collections, and the complete Erba Odescalchi collection.

The museum preserves numerous works originating from the diocese, from the sixth to the nineteenth century. Then there are the "Fondi Oro", fourteenth- and fifteenth-century Tuscan works that a private collector donated to the museum, the section dedicated to St. Ambrose, precious metal artefacts, the cycle of paintings commissioned by the Santissimo Sacramento archconfraternity, and the *Via Crucis* by Gaetano Previati. Twentieth-century works will be added in the future, but for the time being there is a lack of suitable space. Nevertheless, several works by twentieth-century masters – including Aldo Carpi and Lucio Fontana – are displayed.

Sant'Eustorgio, Portinari chapel, interior; the main dome.

Francesco Hayez, Crucified Christ with the genuflected, weeping Magdalene, 1827. Museo Diocesano.

Antwerp workshop, Passion altarpiece, mid-sixteenth century. Diocesan Museum.

The Darsena Dock and Navigli Canals

Piazza XXIV Maggio, with the Darsena dock facing one side, is just a short distance from Sant'Eustorgio. The Darsena is the confluence basin of the two surviving branches of Milan's canal network, namely the Naviglio Pavese and the Naviglio Grande.

The Navigli towpaths have become the location of dozens of cafés and sports clubs. As a result, they are always crowded, especially in the summer when roads are closed to traffic, making them the perfect place for a delightful stroll. On the last Sunday of the month, enthusiasts and collectors of bric-a-brac and antiques flock to approximately 200 stalls selling a variety of these items along the streets.

Vicolo dei Lavandai, at the top of Naviglio Grande, has long wooden canopies that cover the wash houses, the only surviving remnant of late-nineteenth-century working class Milan.

The Gothic church of San Cristoforo sul Naviglio was founded at the end of the thirteenth century and extended by Gian Galeazzo Visconti in 1398.

The unusual and vibrant architectural structure of the double hall is a delightful example of the Visconti Gothic style, characterized by the external redbrick face. The church and adjacent ducal chapel boast of a wealth of paintings, as well as a large wooden statue of St. Christopher with the Christ Child.

Vicolo dei Lavandai, Naviglio Grande.

San Cristoforo, late thirteenth century.

Spanish Walls and Porta Romana

Construction of the city walls began in 1545, but the walls were almost entirely demolished in the late nineteenth century to construct the ring roads. The chief relic of the famous Spanish bastions is gate of Porta Romana, erected at the end of the sixteenth century and embellished with bas-reliefs, plaques and a sturdy architectural framework. A surviving stretch of walls can be seen along Viale Filippetti, just a short distance from the city gate.

Fragments of Spanish walls.

Porta Romana, late sixteenth century.

New Architecture

Teatro degli Arcimboldi

Until 2004, the year the restoration of La Scala is scheduled to be finished, this venue hosts the company that usually performs in Piermarini's building. It is a typical theatre, the type of building that comes to mind when one thinks of a theatre: in short it is a place where "listening is the star of the show". This is how architect Vittorio Gregotti expressed the objectives that guided his work, undertaken in 1996, in designing the Teatro degli Arcimboldi alla Bicocca. The theatre opened in January 2002.

Incorporated in the Bicocca Project designed by Vittorio Gregotti, the building has an independent architectural identity and is located between the city centre and the Milan metropolitan area. Consequently, the theatre serves both the city centre and the suburbs.

In the Arcimboldi Theatre, the dimensions, the profile of the ceiling, the choice of wood for the walls, floor and moving panels, the use of glass sheets for diffusing light and regulating acoustics, are the outcome of successful mediation between formal requirements and technical solutions.

Though simple materials have been used, the entrance is bright and welcoming. The theatre has been designed to generate the interplay of views among the spectators, seated on various levels. At the same time, it also creates more intimate spaces, as occurs when crossing the upper foyer in direct contact with the enormous sloped window. The Arcimboldi Theatre seats 2400 spectators, who benefit from an extensive stall area split into two interconnected levels and with two sets of projecting circles.

The external shell is marked by the play of simple volumes, which delineate the formal clarity of the interior arrangement of the entrance and foyer, stalls, circles, stage and understage.

Teatro degli
Arcimboldi.

The Bovisa District

The Bovisa was established in the suburbs northwest of Milan during the second half of the 1800s as the site of the Candiani chemical industries along Strada Bovisasca. Its development over the years has been highly original. In a very short period of time, railways, gasworks, hospitals, and large and small industrial plants were constructed alongside or over the fields.

Industrial growth and urban transformation continued over the years, but these developments were rarely taken into account in urban planning. Interest in these suburbs started to grow in the 1960s, when the de-industrialization process began and factories cut the number of employees, halving the workforce.

After analyzing Bovisa's potential, in 1987 the Polytechnic Council chose the area as the site of the new university. In 1989 the Bovisa Campus of the Milan Polytechnic Institute was opened in a converted industrial shed. This was the starting point for the Grande Bovisa project, of which part of the Faculty of Engineering and the

second faculty of Architecture are already active. This plan for the active recovery of the city's industrial heritage includes a project to reutilise the two gasworks, constructed in about 1906 by a London-based factory. The structures will become the site of Milan's Museum of the Present.

There are many other projects for this area, which was long considered a "vacant site". Thus, the area's appearance is destined to change dramatically, and Bovisa will become an important part of the city.

Faculty of Engineering buildings at Milan Polytechnic's Bovisa campus.

Fiera di Milano

Milan hosts one of the largest exhibition districts in Europe. It consists of 26 pavilions, with a gross total exhibition area of 348,000 square metres (nearly 3.8 million sq. ft), with additional space of 2000 square metres (over 21,000 sq. ft) of space for non-exhibition purposes. The most recent intervention dates back to the second half of the 1990s with the construction of three new pavilions (14, 15, 16) in the "Portello" area. These structures provide service equipment and state-of-the-art logistical solutions. In addition, there are four fashion show rooms, 27 screening rooms and 38 conference rooms, which can host from 20 to 2000 people.

These rooms include twelve ultramodern rooms in the multipurpose centre, created recently by renovating Pavilion 17.

Milan Trade Fair.

The new pavilions in the "Portello" area, designed by Mario Bellini.

Armani Theatre by Tadao Ando

The Spring/Summer 2002 fashion show inaugurated the new theatre in the former Nestlé factory, which has become the headquarters of the great Italian fashion designer Giorgio Armani. The space was completely reorganized by Tadao Ando, the Japanese minimalist architect. In designing the theatre, Ando pinpointed a line starting at the entrance and spanning the entire depth of the building. This route is underscored by two long walls and a colonnade leading to the foyer, defined by a curved concrete wall. Inside, the theatre is an open space distinguished by its great flexibility.

Fashion shows and performances are staged there, and the theatre is so big that Giorgio Armani can organize a single session for his fashion show. Previously, his fashion shows had to be staggered when they were held at the small theatre on Via Bergognone.

Tadao Ando, former Nestlé factory, the site of the Armani Theatre.

Tadao Ando, Armani Theatre, the foyer.

Translations
Globe, Foligno

Graphic Coordination
Dario Tagliabue

Editorial Coordination
Cristina Garbagna

Layout and Editing
Globe, Foligno

Technical Coordination
Paolo Verri
Mario Farè

Photographic references

Photography by Paolo Manusardi/Electa, Milan

Sergio Anelli/Archivio Electa, Milan
Mauro Ranzani/Archivio Federico Motta Editore, Milan
Paolo Biraghi, Milan
Luigi Ciminaghi, Milan
Civica Raccolta delle Stampe Achille Bertarelli, Castello
Sforzesco, Milan
Civiche Raccolte d'Arte applicata del Castello Sforzesco, Milan
Civico Museo degli Strumenti Musicali del Castello
Sforzesco, Milan
Galleria d'Arte Moderna, Milan
Museo d'Arte Contemporanea, Collezione Jucker, Milan
Museo Bagatti Valsecchi, Milan
Museo Diocesano, Milan
Museo Poldi Pezzoli, Milan
Museo Teatrale alla Scala, Milan
Olympia Publifoto, Milan
Pinacoteca Ambrosiana, Milan
Studio Fotografico Azzurro
Veneranda Fabbrica del Duomo, Fototeca, Milan

Courtesy Ministero per i Beni e le Attività Culturali:
Soprintendenza per il Patrimonio Storico Artistico
e Demoetnoantropologico per le Province di Milano,
Bergamo, Como, Lecco, Lodi, Pavia, Sondrio, Varese

Soprintendenza per i Beni Architettonici e per il Paesaggio
di Milano

www. electaweb.it

This volume was printed for Mondadori Electa S.p.A. at Martellago
Mondadori Printing S.p.A., Via Castellana 98, Martellago (Venice) in 2004